Introduction

Have you ever felt like everyone else is living your dream?

For as long as I can remember, I thought being successful was doing what you were "suppose to" do.

But in 2011, all of the "suppose to's" let me down. I started doing it my way and leveraging the power of social media and that dream to make it happen.

You can too.

Through leveraging social media you can:

Create a freedom based business where you do the work you feel called to do and that lights you up, have more time and flexibility to be with your family, to travel and enjoy life; all while bringing in an incredible income!

I'm taking this message globally through this book "Ideas Worth Stealing: 35 social media strategies that build a brand, share your story and increase sales."

But this isn't JUST about a book... this is about a worldwide movement of women everywhere stepping up and stepping into the life they want to have.

In this moment, the dream that you are holding onto is possible.

In this book you'll find solid strategies that lead to results on your P&L.

Like you, I'm a small business owner who started this company from scratch. There's blood, sweat and tears behind it all. Because I know that mindset, I know that you just want to know what works and what you can be doing to grow your business. The no fluff ASSET System contains five parts and I'm inviting you to steal my process.

Alignment: Sync your online marketing strategy with your business objectives and traditional marketing efforts.

Significance: Maximize results by allocating social where and when it makes sense in your marketing.

System: Line up your resources and leverage your tools the way top social brands do to make more impact.

Engagement: Strengthen the core of your social success by using best practices that get customers involved.

Training: Educate and encourage your team to be actively involved in your online marketing and sales initiative.

Social Marketing, Social PR, Online Marketing or Social Media Marketing--it doesn't matter what you call it, it just matters that you want to get real results. If that's the case, this book is for you.

-Katrina Padron

Alignment:

Sync your online marketing strategy with your business objectives and traditional marketing efforts.

Too often I hear about increasing Likes and increasing followers, but what about increasing sales?

The most effective way to start your online strategy is to identify what result you want. Align social media marketing with your business goals for the most effectiveness.

If you want more sales, these might be goals that you have.

- Increase website traffic

- Increase repeat sales

- Obtain more press

- Grow exposure or reach

- Obtain a higher sales average

Social Media Marketing can accomplish all of those goals. You just need to align your strategy to do so.

Is Social Worth the Investment?

Remember when your mom used to ask, "If your friends did something silly would you do that too?"

Things probably changed since then and you notice that it can be harder to convince people to get on board with you when it comes to social media's investment of time and money.

These are 5 reasons why social marketing done well is worth you company's time and money.

Trust: People don't necessarily trust advertisements and they resent advertisers for interrupting their day. Having conversations and building relationships achieves the opposite effect. People are open to it and engage when they have time.

Visibility: With your target market spending an average of 23 minutes four times a day on social media sites you have an opportunity for more exposure. This exposure is from potential customers and from media looking for stories.

Word of Mouth: Word of mouth is the most preferred marketing tool for small businesses. It takes just a second for someone to share content about your brand with their friends, family and other like-minded people.

Voice: As the publisher of your content, you get more say in what people hear about you and your brand.

Cost: Cost starts at zero. Although you can pay for graphics, photography and video production most content will be very low cost.

Promote Profitable Items

It's right back to the basics, but before you start any promotion you need to know what to promote and how it's going to impact your bottom line. With the over abundance of the deal-of- the-day sites that give away the farm and fall short when it comes to repeat business, you'll want to be confident in the margins of any item or special offer that is promoted.

Start by taking the Product Engineering concept to find your products or services that are a star, dog, challenge or workhorse. The calculation takes into consideration product cost percentages, contribution margins and accounts for popularity.

Star: Both profitable and popular.

Dog: Unprofitable and unpopular.

Challenges: Profitable but relatively unpopular.

Workhorses: Relatively unprofitable but popular.

This is how you'll evaluate which items are best in promotions; you will know what you want to sell.

Once those items are determined plan to promote those items more heavily than the others.

Remember, promotion doesn't always mean discount so you can take a picture of the item coming out of a newly shipped box, being packaged, being displayed, demonstrated, worn or paired with another matching item! There's so much you can do with one single item to highlight it without offering a discount.

Goof Proof Plan to Get Past Customers to Come Back More Often

Radian 6/Salesforce estimates it cost 5-10 times more to bring in a new customer than it does to retain a past customer. That startling number is the exact reason why this step is crucial to your success.

Take an inventory of the systems and databases you are already using. This includes things like your shopping cart, email platforms and your point of sale system.

When customers come to your brick and mortar, your staff needs to be trained to ask for the customers' email address and ask for permission to send them promotional offers and relevant information. Some retail brands are doing great with this by offering to email the receipt to the customer. From there it's as simple as checking a box, exporting the file and importing it into your email system.

Most brands send emails once or twice a month and have average open rates of 20%. They also see an increase in unsubscribes when emails are sent more than 1 time per week. Customers are raising their hand, saying they are fans and they want to build relationships with you and your brand. The easy solution is to continue sending your promotional emails but provide value on your social sites too.

Success Stories:

Within a month of working with us, Make My Notebook started seeing consistent sales daily and the average order price on those sales increased.

The Machine Shed Restaurant ran a recipe book promotion by emailing their current list the link to download a free copy of the book and used fan gating on Facebook to grow Facebook Fans from zero to 5,000 in one quarter.

Strings Restaurant compiled five recipes into "Secrets of a Strings Chef" and sent the email to their current list. The result was that they doubled their Facebook Fans overnight and increased their daily engagements by 50%.

Once those databases are merged you now have a platform to invite customers to come back more often and a platform to invite customers to join you on your social sites too.

What you can do right now is circle one day of each month to export the email addresses from your shopping cart software and import them into your email system.

LinkedIn for Sales

Many brands are reporting surges in sales, fueled by revived corporate spending.

Wholesale accounts are appealing to many brands and there are many off line ways to increase sales but the most effective online strategy to bring in wholesale leads and sales is to leverage LinkedIn.

When most people think of LinkedIn they think of job searching, recruiters and posting a resume. In spite of that, "LinkedIn generates more leads for B2B companies than Facebook, Twitter or blogs." - Social Media B2B

These are the exact steps to bring in wholesale leads on LinkedIn.

- Make sure that your profile is complete and top notch. Include a great headshot of you smiling, headline that stands out and makes clear what you do, many connections and endorsements to build trust and credibility.

- Identify your target market's title, keywords, location and organizations.

- Join the groups that your target market is a member of. For example, if your target market is a boutique owner, go to Search Groups and type "boutique." When the results come up join groups that are active and have large followings.

- On the Group page, select "Members" and a list of all members will populate. Refine the search by specifying geographic location or specific job title within the members section and a targeted list will populate.

- Send a magnetic message by hovering over their profile. When it turns blue and send message button will appear. Click that and write a subject line and paste your Magnetic Message. Your Magnetic Message will be 5

sentences with these specific components.
- o Sentence 1 and 2 will be about them, their vision, a mutual connect or something you have in common.
- o Sentence 3 and 4 will be about what you've done for other people like them.
- o Sentence 5 is the call to action.

Go ahead and work off this sample.

Subject Line: Products

Hello Kathleen,

I noticed you own an adorable boutique in Denver and noticed that you are focused on offer unique hand-made products by local artisans.

Our products have been getting praise by Sunset Magazine and lifestyle bloggers for being just that: unique and handmade with love.

Kathleen, I'd love to see our products in your store. I'm happy to discuss this week, but in the meantime take a look at our wholesale kit here (link).

All the best,

Katrina

In your message make sure it is clear what they need to do next. The best next step is have them click a link that takes them to an email opt in form. This way, you'll be able to track how many people clicked the link and you'll be capturing their email address for upcoming wholesale email campaigns.

Once your team receives their email you can directly contact them with a warm call.

LinkedIn Company Page for Wholesale Sales

LinkedIn is a powerful lead generation and sales platform for companies that use it properly. Engaging with your ideal target market is simple and you'll be reaching your B2B target market significantly faster than you would on other platforms like Twitter and Facebook.

A LinkedIn Company Page is different than a LinkedIn Profile.

To create your Company Page, visit http://www.linkedin.com/company/add/show.

The next steps are to upload basic information. When that is published, you'll have the option to "Request Recommendations." This sends an email to your loyal customers that you select and asks for them to recommend your brand.

The reason this is powerful is based on their

connections so a couple things are important to know.

We know that people tend to be connected to other like-minded people. If you're a boutique shop owner, you might mingle with a lot of other sales people at networking events.

LinkedIn works the same way. If Elizabeth, a boutique shop owner, carries your products and she recommends your company page as a high quality product provider who is reliable, then all of her connections will see that too.

If you are not already connected on LinkedIn with many of your loyal customers or wholesale accounts you can send them a personal email with the link to recommend your restaurant. This will get the ball rolling from the get go.

The next step is to post content and appealing offers to this page. The best way to do this is to think of what your ideal B2B prospect might want or need.

What can you offer that speaks to that mind frame?

When you create this content be certain that it includes a call to action to let the reader know exactly what they can do get more information or place an order.

When you post this content post it on your LinkedIn Company Page so that people who follow your company will see it.

Then, take it one step further. Go into your "groups" and post your content or offer on each of the group pages whose members would be interested in that content. This will get your content in front of more prospects quickly.

Get Your Ducks in a Row

Something about reading a new book makes us want to start fresh. We reach for the clean slate and make new plans. It's an exciting time of the year but there are a few things to do first so that you know exactly where you stand before you make your new spot-on plans.

1. Claim Your Pages: Most brands have many rogue pages living online. These pages may have been created by well intending staff members but were later abandoned or they may have been created by customers checking in to your location. Either way, it's time that you claim them as yours. This gives you the ability to merge with your current page if it is a duplicate or you can keep the page instead of starting from scratch if you do not have a page on that platform yet.

2. Google Yourself: The first thing people do when they hear your name or company name is Google it. We all do it, but do you know what comes in the search results? Give it a try!

3. Do a Source Search: Knowing what content is already popular on your site can really steer you in a direction that will help you get more exposure. A favorite tool for this is to see what people are already pinning from your site. Just type this url http://pinterest.com/source/padronsocialmarketing.com, but of course swap out my url for yours.

4. Check Search Inquiries: Similar to a Source Search on Pinterest, this search tells you what people are searching for on your site. If there is a popular search that you don't have content for, it is the perfect opportunity to create popular content and to rank higher on Google.

5. Do a Keyword Search: Knowing what people are searching for helps you pinpoint your content strategy. The most simplistic way to do this is access Google's Keyword Tool. You'll look for keywords and phrases with a high amount of searches and low competition.

6. Look at Your Open Rates: Right in the same vein check out what's been popular content from your email marketing efforts.

7. Know Your Analytics: Google has a suite of helpful tools for small businesses. One of these tools is Google Analytics. This shows how many people visit your site, where they come from before they get to your site and what they do on your site.

8. Check Review Sites: There are many review sites out there; the most common are Yelp!, TripAdvisor and Urbanspoon. Take a look at those sites to see what people are saying. It's likely there are positive and negative reviews. The negative reviews are a great way to find areas to improve!

9. Do a Related Search: This one is fun! It's always helpful to know what your competitors are (and aren't) doing. Pull up a Google search page and type related:yoursite.com (example: related:padronsocialmarketing.com). When you click search, Google will pull up pages that are similar to yours. I mostly use this when I'm looking for blogs to pitch and companies to partner.

10. List Influencers: Influencers are powerful. These are people who are already in front of your target market. People (and your target market) are spending hours a day online. What blogs, websites, thought leaders, brands, local

pages and celebrities does your audience already follow? These are influencers for your brand! The action step is to put them on a Twitter list and a Facebook list so that it is simple to engage with them frequently.

11. **Invite Email Subscribers:** It's no surprise that I love email and it's still very powerful. People on your list have already raised their hand to say that they love your brand and they want to hear more! Fan gating content on your Facebook page and inviting your email subscribers to get the content will no doubt increase your Facebook fans with quality prospects.

12. **Set Up Monitoring:** There are millions of tweets and posts going live non-stop. In your Hootsuite account, add a panel that searches for your keywords. Include your name, your company name and relevant industry keywords. This will help you know what people are saying about your industry and brand.

13. **Search Tweet Chats:** Tweet chats are a wonderful way to connect with like-minded influencers. This opens the door to joint ventures and gets you in front of their audience too.

14. **Subscribe to Alerts:** Another one of Google's

suite of business tools is Google Alerts. When you sign up for this, Google will send you an email whenever there is an article for the topic. I like to set Google Alerts for my name, company name, "Call for Speakers" and industry trends.

Find Your Signature Voice

While I do love vanilla ice cream a vanilla sounding voice doesn't work online. In the world of social media and online marketing there is an avalanche of noise. In order to be found, be heard and be adored your content must break through that noise and say something different.

3 Quick Steps to Find Your Brand's Signature Voice

1. When I started my marketing career in 2006 we used the term brand drivers; some people call this your Unique Selling Proposition (USP) and now most people call it your WHY or your One Thing. No matter what you call it, it is the reason people buy your product over a competitor's voice. It's the thing that drives them to choose your brand. If you aren't sure what this is yet, start a brainstorming list and fill in the blank to these

questions.

- The thing I'm most passionate about is _____.
- When it comes to my industry, the one thing people need to know is _____.
- The thing that drives me crazy is _____.
- In our industry, we are the only ones confident enough to say
- _____.
- If I could tell people one thing about my industry it would be _____.

2. One of the best pieces of advice I've been given to find a solution to my problem is to look outside of my own industry. When we look for inspiration within our industry we'll often find many people doing a similar thing. When we look outside of our industry we'll find new things to inspire us: new business models, new ways to package goods and new ways to reveal our brands. You'll find so much inspiration online that I recommend organizing it onto a Pinterest board. That way you can always come back to it.

3. In the era we live in, we Google everything! Of course I love that, but another way to draw inspiration and find your voice is to look offline. Take a walk downtown and look at flyers. What speaks to you? Head to a gift store and look at stationary. Do you love the way certain greeting cards are worded? Flip through a few magazines at the grocery store. Did you find something the feels like it's part of your voice? Watch your favorite TV show and jot down notes when words or phrases stand out to you!

Take all of your inspiration from these three questions, pull it together and you'll have a signature voice that stands out from the crowd.

5 Keep in Your Back Pocket Secrets for Profitability

"Sometimes you win, sometimes you learn."

I've been in business for 2 years and I'm constantly learning. The best part is that I'm thrilled to share with you a few shortcuts so you can jump right to winning!

1. Lead with Benefits: It can be hard to see but there's a distinct difference between selling features and selling benefits. Features are what your product or service does and

benefits are your value. In my industry, social media and online marketing, many of my competitors sell their features. They tell clients that they will post on Facebook 3 times a day and increase fans by 1000. That is wonderful but it fails to convey the benefit. The benefit comes from the client's pain and the feature like this. We will strengthen your brand, deliver web traffic to your sales page and sell out your events! See the difference?

2. Find Your Niche: When you're just starting, there's this universal inclination to target everybody because that seems better than potentially excluding someone that could possibly be interested in your service at some point in their life, but the more you narrowly focus your sales and marketing efforts the more easily clients will come on board. Clients will come on board more easily because you're the known expert for what that type of person needs, your language and copy speak directly to them instead of broad general strokes and your case studies demonstrate exactly what you can do for them.

3. Negotiate on Behalf of Others: Recently, I attended a conference called Startup Phenomenon and a brilliant Stanford professor, Margaret Neale, spoke about how women view negotiation. My ears perked up because I've never considered myself to be sales savvy or a poised negotiator. The fascinating thing she said is that studies show that women have a difficult time negotiating for themselves but when women are asked to negotiate for others they out-perform men every time! You know what I did the next day? With every sales conversation I had I removed myself. It's not about me; I now have the sales conversation on behalf of my family, my employees and the non-profits that I donate to. Suddenly, a new type of confidence came into my life and negotiation became easy!

4. Build a Team (even when you're not ready): Even when you don't think you have enough revenue coming in it is pretty likely that you can creatively figure out a solution that will take tasks off your plate so you can focus in your zone of genius. The big thing to keep in mind here is to mitigate risk. For this reason, I

love bringing on part time contractors.

5. Build Relationships: If you've heard it once, you've heard it a million times, but my burning question was "HOW?" How do you build relationships with professionals who you'd like help from? The answer is to give. Go on LinkedIn and give them a recommendation. Give them an article you came across that you thought would be beneficial to them. Give them a referral. Say congratulations when you see they've been featured somewhere, brought on a new client or partnered with another company.

Significance:

Maximize results by allocating social where and when it makes sense in your marketing.

You don't have to so it all. Doesn't that feel good to hear? And, it feels good knowing that this is the truth. You only need to do what you think is best for your business and what will give you the best results. That's it.

With that said, in this section there are tactics for being highly targeted in your efforts.

Get Going with Google Offers

Free samples is a great way to win friends. Giving out a little sample is the best but that's not always possible, especially if your potential customer is still a few miles away.

Google has a powerful tool for that. It's Google Offers.

Go to your Google Local Business Dashboard. http://www.google.com/business/placesforbusiness/

In your listing click "Offers." Then click the red button that says "Add New Offer."

Next, you'll be promoted through simple steps to build your offer including the Design, Availability and Redemption, and Additional Restrictions.

Submit the offer and your potential customers who are searching on Google for this type of product in your area will see the offer.

To redeem the offer, the customer will show their phone to your staff member and the staff member will select the Google Offer button you create in your POS.

*Be sure servers are trained to expect this type of

coupon and trained to ring it in.

Celebrate with Birthday Offers

I'm known to use cliches and really dated phrases. One that I use too often is *fish when the fishing is good.*

Birthdays are a time when the fishing is good. We know that people in our culture love birthdays and are going to do something special to treat themselves and celebrate.

This is a perfect time for you to encourage them to buy your product, but you might be wondering how you would know their birthday and how you could do that.

You don't need to know their birthday. Facebook already knows it.

Your first step is to post an image of your product that would be a perfect way for them to treat themselves on their birthday or post a graphic with a special offer they can use during their birthday week. Write a line of text that is 90 characters or less so plan ahead and then paste in a short link to your offer page so that customers will immediately be redirected to download the offer.

Once it's live on your Facebook page, go into the Facebook Advertising Panel https://

www.facebook.com/advertising and "Create an Ad."

Select your business' Facebook page as your destination. Click Promote Page Post. On the drop down that appears select your Birthday Post.

In the targeting section, select age and gender. Use what you already know about your target market here. Who is most likely to buy?

Now is the fun part! In the Broad Categories section select Events. To the right of that select "Has a birthday within a week." (That means your ad will only show up to people who are 1. in your target market and 2. have a birthday within a week). You can make your ad even more targeted by adding precise interest. These are brands, organizations, associations and public figures that your target market feels affinity toward.

For this, I recommend the default settings for Connections.

Under Campaign, Pricing and Schedule follow these steps. Name your campaign something that will let you know what it is. For pricing, you can select a number that feels right to you and your P&L. Set your start and end dates. Let it at least run for a few weeks so you can get your promotion out there and also give people time to come in to celebrate. For pricing select for Facebook Optimization.

Place order and usually in a few hours your ad will be up and running.

Bonus Tip: Follow the same steps but target people who just moved to your neighborhood by selecting "Recently Moved" in the Broad Category: Events section.

Avoid Losing Easy Targets

When someone signs up for your email newsletter they are raising their hand and saying "I'm interested in your business." They like you and they are an easy target to funnel to your Facebook Page.

Use this two step process to get them to like your Facebook page. Yep, its just two steps.

1. Put this simple statement on your email Welcome letter. "Don't forget to complete your membership, 'Like' (your business name) on Facebook."
2. Then, copy and paste the link to your Facebook page.

That's it.

You have one more way to stay in front of potential

customers and increase your repeat purchases.

Facebook vs. Twitter

What do you think? Which social network is the best for business?

There are hundreds of social media networks your business could be on. Hundreds of business owners get stuck on that. They don't know which one to be on and feel like if they are not everywhere, then they must be missing potential clients and customers.

That's not the case.

There are 2 things (yes, just 2) that you need to consider when you are using social media to market your business.

It's my most straightforward advice and I'll tell you exactly what they are.

1. Where are your customers spending most of their time? The key to online marketing is to be in front of your customers where they are already spending time so that you don't have to waste time and energy hunting for them.

2. Use what you're comfortable with. If something is exceptionally difficult, confusing

or simply time consuming for you, it'll never get checked off your to do list. If you love a platform (like many of us find with Pinterest), it won't even feel like work.

Kickstart Your Campaign

So you have big news! You've been hard at work over the past few weeks creating something pretty special. It's a new product and it's going to rock!

But wait, no one knows about it. Have you been there? Ready to tell everyone about your new "thing," but had no idea who to do it?

Follow these 3 steps to Kickstart Your Campaign.

1. Let everyone on your email list know what you're up to. Use these 6 key elements in your email.
    - Write your 'can't pass up' headline.
    - Write your attention grabbing opener.
    - Share your story/reason for the message.
    - Explain what you are offering.
    - Describe what's in it for them.
    - Give clear concise directions for how to respond with a call to action. Common ones are Buy Now, Enroll Here, Get the Goods Here, Try Now, Subscribe Here and Click for Instant Access.

2. Schedule advanced praise. You want your launch to be strong from the get go. Scheduling advance praise will generate excitement leading up to the launch and will put you in front of other people's subscribers/readers/followers/fans. Start by making a list of people who have a similar target customer. They can be your competitor or they can be in a completely different industry but this works best when their target customer is someone who would be interested in your product. Craft an email like this.

Hi <blank>,

I've been hard at work over the past few weeks creating something pretty special. It's a new product and it's going to rock!

I am sending my special product to a micro-handful of amazing people, in the hopes of gathering advance reactions, reviews, praise, feedback & general applause.

I'm launching on <date>, which is <number of days> from today. So if there's anything you'd like to share, please give it to fast.

THANK YOU for your support.

<your name>

1. Generate more excitement with pre-feed praise and affiliates. Big successful launches generally have a lot of people supporting the launch. Pre-Feed Praise and an outstanding affiliate program will get other people spreading the word about your product for you. This is meaningful because other people will be getting behind you, supporting your work and telling others how great it is. It also spreads your message to people that would otherwise be out of your reach.

Again, start by crafting an email to people that would be great people to promote your product. Design an email like this.

Hey <fan's name>,

I hope you thoroughly enjoyed your sneak-peek at my product. It was a joy to create, and I'm revving up for a big launch.

Want to help me spread the love?

I've got a handful of ready-to-go tweetables that you can copy & paste, straight into your social media feed.

And better yet...become an affiliate for the product and include a shortened version of your affiliate link, whenever you tweet, post or toss your praise around.

You'll earn <number of dollars> for every click-through sale, *plus my unbelievable amounts of appreciation.*

CLICK HERE to enroll, and email me at <email> if you need any help at all.

Your support means to world to me. Thank you so much, <fan's name>. <your signature>

7 Common Internal Marketing Mistakes and What to Do Instead

Things are constantly changing. Social Media and Online Marketing best practices are constantly changing and what used to work might not work on your next campaign.

Let's go through the top 7 mistakes that internal marketing teams commonly make and what to do instead.

- Overlooking Integration Opportunities: Salesforce.com says it costs 5-10 times more to attract new guests than it does to retain past guests. Many small businesses are already using 2 platforms that when used to a full potential can seamlessly help your business retain past customers.
    - The first platform is your shopping cart. Each time someone buys your product, the shopping cart collects their contact

information. The best thing to do with this information is to make sure that it's imported into your email communication system so that these people are receiving your content too.

- o That brings us to the second piece-- email marketing. Once the emails are in Mailchimp or another email marketing platform create content that your database can only download through Facebook. This is called fan gating and it means that you are offering something of value (i.e. a coupon or content) that you will give to your customer in exchange for them hitting like on your Facebook page. The easiest and free platform to set up a fan gate is http://www.woobox.com

- Leaving Out Community Sites: Planning special events like an open house, grand openings and product launches is a fantastic way to attract new customers. Of course in marketing these events your team will be using email marketing, posting on social networks and maybe placing paid advertising, but many small businesses miss the opportunity to put promotional information on larger community sites. These are sites will a larger audience than you have and almost every city has something like this. It might be a Go and Do Magazine or a What's Hot Local Blog. Do a little research and ask around because they are out there and can be a wonderful way to get more traffic.

- Including Only Facebook and Twitter in Your Social Strategy: Social Times says 61% of users use LinkedIn as their primary professional network, 35% of LinkedIn users access it daily and Social Media B2B says LinkedIn generates more leads for B2B companies than Facebook, Twitter or blogs. Two fantastic ways to use LinkedIn for B2B sales is to collect wholesale leads and press leads. You'll need to develop an attraction email, drill down on your target market and send messages inviting your target to take the next step.

- Missing Opportunities to Increase Search Rankings: A recent study says that 64% of mobile restaurant searchers convert immediately or within an hour. That's an unbelievable number and what that means to you is that when they search (whether they are using Google+ Local, Facebook Nearby, Yelp!, TripAdvisor or UrbanSpoon) your small business needs to show up and look good. It sounds like a first date, but it's that simple!

- Let's start with the look good piece of that. Of course you'll want basic information about your brand, hours and photography to be current, accurate and appealing, but you also want your reputation to look fantastic too. This requires you to claim each of your pages, address negative reviews and thank people for positive reviews. Another little integration trick here is to email past customers to offer an incentive for them taking the time to review your product. Include the link and then send their incentive after they post the review.

- The second piece of increasing search rankings is to have highly active back links, content and citations. A business page with posts that have few likes, comments and content feels a bit like an empty bar; you got to fill it in order to bring in more passer-bys!

• Promoting Low Profit Items: Facebook Offers (and the still present check-in-deals) are fantastic ways to create behavioral change and get guests to come to your restaurant. I'm not a fan of deal a day programs, but what I love about offers and check in deals is that it gives guests an opportunity to sample your products and your experience but here's the key ingredient you need to know. Pull a product mix report and analyze what your most popular and profitable items are. Essentially you'll be analyzing the popularity and profitability of an item. Choose to promote items that are highly popular and high profitable; these are your STARS! This works by creating an offer that will be delivered to your Facebook fanbase, this is why it's important to grow this community. Customers will click to redeem the offer and come to your website to buy it.

- Down Sourcing to Interns: The fresh, young digital natives at your company embody a crucial resource in helping to navigate the emerging media waters. In some cases, however, their lack of business experience could hinder your brand's "social voice." Align your social strategy with current business goals instead of building pages because you want to.

- Having Rouge Pages: It seems there was a time when companies used dummy accounts and fictional characters to untangle the ties between a personal Facebook Profile and a Facebook Business Page and a time when ambitious employees started a company Facebook Page but later left the company without leaving access to the page. Clean those up now so people can find you. Most platforms allow for you to clean up and merge pages. This will strengthen your brand page and will also make it easier for people to find you.

Get a Vanity Url

Have you customized your Facebook username? If you don't even know what that means - no worries its super simple.

A username is what Facebook calls a vanity url. To find out if you've already done this just go to your Facebook and look at the url. Does it say www.facebook.com/a-bunch-of mumbo-jumbo-letters-and-numbers or does it say www.facebook.com/your-business-name?

You want it to say www.facebook.com/your-business-name. This will allow you to easily promote your page and people can easily find it.

To do this, go to your Facebook page and click Edit Page, Update Page Info and then edit Page Address.

It just takes a minute so head there now.

Keep a Pre-Holiday Calendar

The holidays begin many months before the lights are hung. While your emails now are focused around fall, Halloween and giving thanks your real job is to focus on the future– be growing and engaging your list so that you are 100% prepared for the holidays!

Common Themes to Focus On:

- Shop our pre-holiday clearance sale
- Get an early start on ordering holiday cards and decor
- Pre-order the hottest holiday gifts
- Preview our holiday collection
- Sign up for our Christmas catalog
- Create a wish list
- Learn about layaway and other services

Tips for Limited Time Offers

You've seen it.

Get it while you can.

Limited time only.

Offer expires soon!

This is the exact marketing strategy that the sells McDonald's McRib. It's back. Get Yours!

While I'm not a fan of the McRib, I am a fan of creating a sense of urgency for your products and services. It's called a Limited Time Offer (LTO).

My challenge to you is to create a limited time offer that will benefit both your company and your ideal target market by them taking action now.

Common ways to create a mutually beneficial offer is to:

- Help them save money.
- Help them accomplish what they want to have happen.
- Save them time.

Start a little brainstorm list to keep handy and put out there when you need a little sales boost. What would make someone buy now?

7 Do's and Don'ts of Email Marketing

In spite of all the buzz and results companies are getting from social media, email still the workhorse!

Here are 7 Do's and Don'ts of Email Marketing.

- Offer Value in the Subject Line: With 2.8 million emails sent every second, subscribers need to have a reason to open instead of delete.
- Include 1 Call to Action: Readers need to be told what the next step is. Try these. Join now. Sign up now. Click here. Act fast. Share this!
- Stick to 3-4 Fonts and Colors: Keep it simple and well branded. You'll gain top of mind and it'll be easier to read.
- Make it Mobile: Huge percentages of the population (and your target market) are reading their email via their mobile device. You're message will show up clear and optimal with a mobile template.
- Send at Optimal Times: This is different for everyone, but it's at the intersection of when is your target most likely to be able to read your email and when is your competition the lowest.

- Match Your Brand: Use your logo, your brand's voice, your graphics, header and colors.
- Know Your Audience: When you know your audience you can create content that speaks to them and solves their problems. They'll love you for that!

7 High Converting Opt in Offers

You've landed on company websites and seen "Sign up for our monthly newsletter." It's great that they have an opt in box but that offer isn't compelling. It doesn't give a benefit that'll motivate your target to actually sign up and it doesn't really tell your target what to expect.

The simple truth is that it takes work to get a target to your page. A lot of work! If they come to your page and leave without giving their email, it's takes even more work, time and money to reach them and get them to come back again.

Your goal as an online marketer is to get people on your list the first time they visit your site. Otherwise, if people who visit your website aren't jumping on your list before they leave you are missing opportunities to:

1. Build Brand Awareness

2. Increase Sales
3. Lead Generation
4. Strengthen Customer Relationships
5. Reminds Your Customers Who You Are

These are 5 examples of brands that get it right!

1. Big Benefits -Tell your target market what they'll get – not the features but the real benefit.
   a. Ex: Increase your happiness, self-worth and success by downloading over $1,500 in free tools and gifts!
2. Access and Evaluate – Your target market is always interested in tools and knowledge that will help them succeed.
   a. 7 Internal Marketing Mistakes (and what to do instead)
3. Give Guidance – In every industry there are common mistakes that people tend to make. Let your target market know what those are and how to fix them! Shut Up, Sell More!
   a. 10 Things to Never Ever Say in Sales Conversations
4. Take this Quiz – People love to take quizzes, especially when it's about them and it'll help them improve.

    a. Click to Take Actor Type Quiz
5. Teach a Video Course/Series – Give your target market a place to start on the matter. Record videos yourself or invite amazing partners to share their tips too.
    a. PR for Anyone
6. A Take Action Guide – People love step by step guides that clearly state what to do each day.
    a. Daily Action Planner
7. Discount - Great for retail and non-retail brands. We all love a discount!
    a. 10% off your first order!

How to Create an Effective Facebook Cover

No additives. No preservatives. No GMO. We see it all over the grocery store, but when you look at your social strategy is it "no-fluff?"

From the text we write to the images we post, there are key ingredients to make sure what your brand is creating is effective.

When it comes to Facebook Cover Images, the basics are that the size is properly formatted to 851×315 pixels and there is room for your profile picture to overlap but beyond that these are 9 tips for creating an effective Facebook cover image.

1. Utilize Prime Real Estate: You only get a few seconds from the time someone lands on your page to the time they leave or the time they realize they are in the right place and want to stay. Using your cover to clearly state what your company does and provide links to find out more, register for your email newsletter or connect in other places is a great way to get your information in front of these prospects quickly.
2. Highlight Your Service Benefit: Products are extremely easy to highlight, but the service industry tends to overlook this opportunity. Feature your customer's benefit and the results they expect to receive.
3. Tell Your Story: Storytelling is possibly the most effective strategy for growing a brand.
4. Showcase Happy Customers: Nothing sells better than existing customers sharing their enthusiasm for you product or service. You may be collecting text based testimonials but look how appealing photos of happy customers are!
5. Photos of Your Tribe: People are more likely to get involved when they see people like themselves getting involved. If your brand has a tribe of people spreading your message then use the cover image to show this.
6. Make it Current and Relevant: Whether you

have new products for the season or upcoming events, the cover image is a perfect place to showcase timely and relevant happenings for your company.
7. Position Your Image to Go Viral: We love to be a part of something big, something that is changing lives and changing the world. Invite and encourage your tribe to get involved by posting a picture of themselves and tagging their friends in the photo.
8. Include a Strong Call to Action: Someone lands on your page, do they know that next step? What do you want them to do? Where do you want them to go? Say that.
9. Use Creative Graphics: Sharing your brand essence through one graphic is powerful. You know all you need to know just from looking at one image.

Which effective strategies are you going to use?

Collaboration is the New Competition

It's likely that you want to guard your brand and keep some of your secrets safe (and I agree with you). On the other hand, I challenge you to find non-competitive partners with a similar target audience as you and invite them to collaborate on your boards.

Collaboration is crucial these days because it's one of the fastest and lowest cost ways to get exposed to your target market.

Let's walk through an example.

If you own a children's apparel company, then you're likely targeting moms. Tap into that mom's lifestyle and that will help you discover who to partner with: toys, books, advices, packaged food, local play places, blogs she reads, shoe brands, photographers.

Once you have your list of partners, create a collaborative board on Pinterest and invite them to share. Your collaborative board will show on your Pinterest page, but also on your partners' pages too—meaning, their followers will see your pins too.

Must Have's in Every Pin

Just like everything there are certainly best practices on Pinterest too.

Five Things Every Pin Should Have

> 1. Hashtags work the same on Pinterest, Twitter and Facebook. Basically it is a way to categories content that is helpful when people are searching. Think of

what people might search for in order to get this pin to appear and use appropriate hashtags.
2. Links are under-utilized and very powerful. Of course when people click the pin, they will be taken to the link where the image was pinned from but you can also include a link in the description that takes people right to a specific page that you want them to go to.
3. Keyword Rich Description act similar to hashtags, you want your image to show up when people are looking for it. In the caption box write a full and rich description that includes keywords that people would use when they type in the search box.
4. Use proper boards. Many people (especially on mobile) search based on categories (i.e. Women's Fashion, DIY & Crafts, Home Decor, Hair & Beauty, Food & Drink, etc). Pin your content to the appropriate board to make sure you're showing up in there.
5. Putting a price wrapper on a pin is beautifully simple. In the description type a $ and then the numerical value. This is important because if people are

searching for a gift, they can choose their spending range. If your product is within that range, it will appear as a potential gift to purchase.

System:

Line up your resources and leverage your tools the way top social brands do to make more impact.

When I'm experiencing overwhelm and an endless to do list, I generally find that I'm missing a system somewhere. Systems are your savior. With strong systems you'll accomplish more and make a bigger impact.

Secret Sauce to Double Your Fans Overnight

You don't need millions of fans just for the sake of having fans. The reason to want fans is very simple--your posts will show up in their newsfeed.

Now, this might not seem like a very big deal, but these are the 3 benefits of showing up in a fan's newsfeed.

1. Build Top of Mind Awareness: Top of mind is critical for small businesses because studies indicate that a person or household is only loyal to 3-4 brands at a time. You want your brand to be top of mind when someone is in the market.

2. Give Opportunities to Connect: As Fans connect with your brand on Facebook (meaning they like, comment or share), the weight of your posts will be stronger and Facebook will put it in more Newsfeeds. That exponentially expands your reach.

3. Amplify Word of Mouth: Word of Mouth is found to be 50 times more powerful than ads. When a fan interacts with your brand brand on Facebook (meaning they like, share or comment) a "story" of that activity will be

created. That "story" will show up in their friends' Newsfeed, therefore expanding your reach and word of mouth.

Now, do you have a Facebook Page but you really want to grow it for these reasons?

This is the step by step strategy that grew a client's Facebook page from 0-8000 without any paid advertising and doubled another page fans overnight from 1,250-2,500 without any paid advertising.

The Secret Sauce is Fan Gating.

Fan Gating has been around for a while, but the basis is to develop an irresistible piece of content that your customers want then offer it to your email subscribers in exchange for a Like.

You'll need:

1. A link to your irresistible content
2. Bitly link for your fan gate pageCopy written for email
3. Select which app you'll use (my favorite is Woobox)
4. App image 111X74 that is branded
5. Fan Gate Image that says click "Like" in the upper right corner the is no wider than 480

pixels

Step by Step:

1. Upload your irresistible content to your website.
2. Install a Fan Gating app through Woobox.com.
3. Take the link from the fan gate app and make it a bitly link for tracking.
4. Write an email explaining what you're offering and how subscribers can access it. Include the bitly link to the fan gate.
5. Send the email to your subscribers and watch your number of fans increase.

Create Irresistible Content Using Google Analytics

For our wedding we were given a 20 piece knife set from Bed Bath and Beyond. It's awesome! There's this one knife that I use to cut everything, but the other 19 knives just sit there.

That's how Google is too. By far the best platform in the universe for your brand, but unless you're putting some of those tools to use they are just sitting there.

One of my favorite Google tools that most people

don't know about is the Content Reporting feature in Google Analytics. This helps you find your site's top content and hidden gems. This is the content you have that people are searching for, sharing and loving!

When you know what content is strong, you can deliver more of that. The stronger your content is, the stronger your SEO will be and the more traffic will land on your site.

The other tool is Google Commerce Search; this has a reporting feature that lets you understand how your users are using your search engine. You can see reports for the most popular queries, as well as usage statistics over time. When you find out what people are searching for on your website, you find out where the gap is. Develop content to fill that gap.

These two tools together actually give you data for what content you could create that could go viral.

Take a look now!

Rank Higher on Google

Remember your first date? Maybe a little awkward, but your main goal was to show up and look good! The same is true when you customers are searching on Google; you're business needs to show up so they can find you and it needs to look good so they'll choose you.

The easiest way to do this is to claim your Google Place Page. When you claim this page you'll:

1. Show up on Google Search, Maps, Google+, Google Offers and mobile devices.
2. Give customers the right information about your business.
3. Connect with customers by understanding their feedback and responding to reviews.

3 Steps to claim your page.

3. Claim Page: Visit this page and click the get started button.http://www.google.com/business/placesforbusiness/
4. Verify Your Place of Business: You can verify through phone or postcard. If you select the phone option be sure someone is at your business phone, ready to take the call and write down the PIN. If you choose the postcard option be sure that the person receiving the mail in informed to be looking for it.
5. Enter PIN: Once you have your PIN go to the link Google provides you and enter your PIN. Once your' PIN is entered and

successful, you will have access to make changes to your Google Place Page: images, hours, contact info, offers and reviews.

Bad Review Online

Picture this. You jump online and notice that you have a few Facebook notifications. You are excited to see what people are saying so you check it and it's a bad review or a negative comment.

It stinks. It hurts a bit.

But the question is, what do you do? Of course you don't want other people to see it but you also don't want to be the social media police and take down every comment you're not in love with.

This is the step by step.

1. Address the issue with this specific customer. If you want to take the conversation offline simply say something like, "I'm so sorry for your experience. Please email your phone number to [your number] and I am happy to see if I can help. This will show up in your feed and your other prospects and customers will see that you are addressing the problem quickly.
2. Decide whether you want to leave the comment or remove it. It is up to you, but I

generally recommend leaving it simply because it adds an authentic layer to your brand. As a consumer, when we go to pages where customers are only raving and then we have a bad experience, our thought is that this brand must be deleting their negative comments so they look better.

3. Double check to make sure other recent complaints are handled too. Be sure to check sites like Yelp, TripAdvisor and UrbanSpoon (depending on your industry). This can honestly give you so much insight into your business and you can see where issue are coming up.

By looking through reviews you can see if there have been issues regarding the same problem. If you find that to be the case, take is as research and address the issue.

What Big Brands Know About Facebook Engagement Ads

You're ready to use the power of social media, but building a targeted audience takes a long time.

Have you felt like that?

I call this Facebook Frustration. You know there's value, but so far it's been a slow road, not to mention Facebook algorithms are constantly changing and they are confusing us with all of the new features.

I have simple advice that's tried and true for businesses who need and want to build a loyal following quickly and on a tight budget. I'm a believer in Facebook ads.

Facebook Ads put your business in front of your target in a place where they are already spending their time you can craft your ads to reach your ideal audience based on their interest and grow a fan base of ideal customers/clients.

To start, create a post on your page's timeline. The key elements of the post should be: include a clear image that represents what you are offering, the text should be 125 characters or less, include a call to action like "click here" or "sign up now" and a link to where you want your target to go; this might be a page where they can "buy now" or it might be a page where they can sign up for your email list.

Then, go to www.facebook.com/advertsing and click "Create an Ad."

When creating an ad, there is an awesome tool that Facebook offers. They ask you what results you want. The two I use most often are "Get Likes" and "Increase Engagement." For this article, I'm referring to the increase engagement option. When you promote a post to get engagement, Facebook is showing your post that is already on Facebook to more targeted people.

Your bid is based on people clicking Like, adding a comment or sharing the post. The ancillary benefit of using "promote a post" is that prospects will see when their friend interacts with the post. Meaning, if their friend likes, comments or shares your post then the friend who you are targeting will also see that. This will give you more credibility and it will make it more likely that your prospect will engage with the post.

The "promote a post" option will direct you to a drop down menu with all of your latest posts listed. Select the one you just created for this campaign.

Under the Sponsored Stories box put a check mark in all three boxes. This will allow your target to see when other people have liked, commented or shared your post. I love this because it makes social media even more social!

Next, select the basic demographics of your ideal target person: age, gender and geographic location. The more specific you are with your targeting, the better your results will be.

Here's my favorite part of Facebook Ads: precise targeting.

Precise Targeting gives you the ability to laser target your ads. Yes, there are 900 million people on Facebook, but the truth is not all of those people are your target audience and if you are paying for ads, you only want to pay when your ideal target audience clicks on that ad and not when anyone in the world sees your ad.

I'll give you an example of Precise Targeting.

Say I am selling baby clothing. I'm likely selling to moms with young children. So here's what I do. Brainstorm a list of all of the things moms with young children may have Liked on their Facebook Profile: Parenting Magazine, Parents Magazine, American Baby Magazine, Baby Center, Prenatal Yoga, What to Expect When Expecting, Childwise Baby Books, Graco, Pottery Barn Kids, Babies R Us, and Babee Talk. Aim for an audience of 500,000. This will make it so the moms you are targeting have to Like one of the above things in order for them to see you ad.

Let's try a different example. Say you are a graphic designer and your target is branding agencies and pr firms who could outsource work to you. You'll target things like this: PRSA, American Marketing

Association, Colorado American Marketing Association, AdAge, Marketing Power, Seth Godin, Mashable and Social Media Today.

The key is to figure out what magazines your target reads, where they go for coffee, what TV shows they watch, what books they read, what celebrities they follow and what brands they love.

Once you have precise targeting complete go to Campaign, Pricing and Schedule. Give your campaign a title. Then, set your budget. We would all dream to have ad budgets like Coca Cola, but it's unlikely that is the case. The good news about Facebook Advertising is that you can set you Lifetime Budget for each campaign. If you set your Lifetime Budget for $200 then Facebook will stop the campaign at $200 so you never go over. Next, select your date range. You can play with this a bit but I tend to choose shorter time frames so that ads are fresh and continue reaching the right audience.

Generally, I let Facebook optimize my bids for me to start. Facebook's system will adjust your bid as needed to ensure that your ad gets exposure.

Click place order.

In a few hours, usually less, Facebook will email you to let you know if your ad is approved. Most ads will be approved, but if it isn't Facebook will give you the reason and you can go in, make that change and re-submit your order.

Pinterest for Business

Pinterest is hot! But, before we even get to that point I know you're thinking, "I'm on Facebook, Twitter and Google+. Social media already overwhelms me...do I need to be on Pinterest too?" Yes, here's why: Pinterest is referring more web traffic to websites than LinkedIn and Twitter combined!

Pinterest is a virtual pinboard. Pinterest allows you to organize and share all the beautiful things you find on the web. You can browse pinboards created by other people to discover new things and get inspiration from people who share your interests.

Pinterest is gaining enormous traction in just the last couple months. Unique visitors to the site grew 400% from September to December 2011 and it's quickly becoming a favorite tool, especially among the design and retail communities.

With that said, we've found ways to use Pinterest to grow your business and build your brand all while adhering to Pinterest's etiquette.

Quite simply, if you are doing work you would love

to share, pin it; if your work is inspired by someone or something, pin it; if there is something you personally like, pin it. But let me break this down a little more to make sure you are fully leveraging Pinterest.

How to humanize your brand and why it's so important

People like to do business with other people they know, like and trust. Creating boards that show who you are is compelling. It offers a personal side to your business. If you are already using personal branding for your business, use Pinterest to take it to the next level. Use boards to showcase your lifestyle - maybe a "Your Style," "Offices I'd Love to Have," "Best Books List" or "Dream Vacations." These boards help show who you are and give your followers a chance to connect on a personal level with you.

The tip to network with out being pushy and self promotional

Just like any social network, Pinterest is meant to be social. Social media gives you a unique opportunity to get in front of people you might not reach otherwise. You can connect, comment, like and re-pin just as you do on Facebook and Twitter. As you start doing this, you are putting yourself and your business in front of more people. The best way to comment is to be genuine and never self promote in someone else's thread.

What it means to curate content and how to create boards for your target

Curating content means creating boards around a particular idea, category or theme. This becomes even more of an opportunity when you are 100% clear on your target customer. If you know who your target customer is and what they find entertaining, educational and empowering start creating boards that sit in the sweet spot of what they want and what you are an expert on. This helps position you as an expert on that content.

Exactly how to optimize your post for more web traffic

Just last month one study showed that Pinterest drives more visitors to third-party websites than

Google+, YouTube and LinkedIn combined and in many cases Pinterest is driving more web traffic than Twitter. Each pin is a permalink taking people directly to the website where it is from. When you post, be sure the link takes them back to your website where there are opt-in forms or take them to a page where they could purchase, see more items, pin more items or opt in to hear more from you.

Pinterest also wants you include a thoughtful description on your pins. You can include the name of the product, what it was inspired by, price and the link to find it on your website.

The secrets to frictionless sharing on Facebook and Twitter

Pinterest is set for frictionless sharing with Facebook and sharing on Twitter is beyond easy. You likely already have a following on Facebook and Twitter. By sharing your pins directly to those sites you are leveraging your resources and expanding your reach to communities you've already built.

To share directly to Facebook sign onto Pinterest, click your username at the top-right toolbar, then click Edit Profile. Next, you can add/remove Pinterest to your Facebook Timeline by clicking the slider. ON will add your pins to your Facebook Timeline. OFF will remove Pinterest from your Facebook Timeline.

When you are pinning something you will be able to select which board it is pinned to and then in the lower right corner check the Twitter box. That will share the pin directly to your Twitter account.

Overlooked Basics that Could Impact Your Brand

There are so many social networks now, many of us start to overlook the basics. Be sure to make your bio fantastic, use a great profile picture and include links to your website.

2 Ways to Quickly Integrate with Facebook

Like all social media sites we start with zero followers. One way to ramp up your following quickly is to invite your Facebook friends to follow you and follow your Facebook friends. Pinterest has made this really easy.

Click the Invite Friends button in the top right. Then click Facebook in the left margin. Two columns will appear - Invite Friends and Friends on Pinterest. To invite friends, click the red Invite Friends button, select the friends to invite and send requests. To follow friends, click the Follow All button for the Follow button next to their name.

Use the Goodies

It's important to let people know your are on Pinterest so they know to find you there. A simple way to do this is to add a pin it button to your website. People will be able to go straight from your website to your Pinterest account where they can see more about your brand.

Go to Goodies and scroll to "Follow Button" for Websites. There are a few options available. Select the image you would like and Pinterest will generate code. Paste the code into your website.

The other Goodie that makes Pinterest easy and more likely for you to use is the Install a Pin It bookmarklet to your browser. Follow the step by step instructions. If things are easy to pin, you'll be more likely to do it.

How Crowdsourcing Can Feature Your Brand without You Selling It

Ask fans of your brand to pin pictures of themselves with their favorite product of yours and tag you, then you can repin those photos onto a VIP board. It'll show potential customers that your current users really like using your product and it will help build a relationship with your current customers.

Little Known Ways to Optimize Your Pins

Put keywords and hashtags in each description as it relates to your product or service. Users will be more likely to find your pin when searching for something specific if it is optimized. You could put #design #print #damask #wallpaper for a pin about wallpaper.

Search for pins from your company

Pinterest is active and there is a little trick for seeing what people are pinning about your company. Just type this into the url http://pinterest.com/source/padronsocialmarketing.com/ and a list of pins from your website will appear.

This gives great research and insight into what is popular and can help direct some of your efforts, so keep an eye on it. It also allows you to comment back to people from one place.

Social Media Secrets for Sold Out Events

You know that feeling when you see something really cool in action? You see it unfold right before you. Recently, I had the incredible opportunity to attend an event in NYC, and I saw social media and online marketing used so smartly to sell out an event with zero seats to spare and to create an enormous amount of buzz for next year's event.

This is what every business needs to know about using social media for a sell-out event, including getting the word out in the first place, strategies for engaging your audience and how to create momentum afterward.

Before the Event

1. Have a First-to-Know List — Build excitement before details are announced by creating an email opt-in form and encouraging people to get on the First-to-Know List.
2. Hold a contest — Make it big and generate buzz with a contest set to go viral. Tell participants to enter by submitting an article or video below your blog post and encourage them to tweet, comment, share and like by giving bonus points for social media activity. Also, require each post to have your hashtag, official URL to learn more about the event and your Twitter handle.
3. Take a pre-event survey — After registering for the event, send a survey asking your participants what they want to get from the event.
4. Build excitement — Every day leading up to the event, send an assignment/countdown full of content, things to do and encouraging messages.
5. Blog about it — Anything that requires money generally requires your target to talk it over with their spouses/significant others.
6. Create a hashtag for the event and be present in the conversation.
7. Create a Twitter list of who is attending and encourage communication and relationship

building before the event.
8. Create Tweetables to make it easy to share. Click to Share has a great platform for this.
9. Get your speakers excited — Send out an email with your speakers' Twitter handles and ask participants to follow speakers on Twitter.

During the Event

- Ask for live tweets — Tell people to post questions or just post that they are at your amazing event. It's so simple, and people will do it.
- Take photos — During the event, have professionals take photos live and post them to Flickr Live Stream. Tell participants where to find the photos and give them permission to tag themselves and share the pictures on their social networks.
- Get candid testimonials instantly — Nothing sells like a real person telling you how incredible something is while they are experiencing it. During breaks, have designated areas for participants to share their stories and experiences. Capture them and use them in next year's campaign.
- Give a gift — Give a notebook or something valuable that participants will continue to use after they've gone home — something that

will remind them about their incredible experience.

After the Event

1. Give even more — Send emails with an event wrap-up, highlights and additional resources and notes from the speakers. Make it an easy-to-download zip file.
2. Get feedback — Post an event survey right away while details are fresh. Compile critiques and ideas into a list and implement them during your next event.

Invite Networks

One of the biggest complaints I hear about social media marketing is that there are so many platforms and business owners don't know just where to put their resources (see Twitter vs Facebook for more on that), but one way to jump over that hurdle is to integrate as much as you can.

One way to integrate is to invite your current email list or Facebook fans to follow you on Pinterest. After all, they already raised their hand to say the like you and want to hear from you.

2 Easy Ways to Invite Your Network to Pinterest

- Email them letting them know what awesome

and appealing content they can expect by following you on Pinterest.
- Post an image from your Pinterest board to Facebook. Be sure to include the link so they can click to see more and follow you.

Do More of What Works

The first time I ever heard K.I.S.S. (Keep it Simple, Stupid) was in my freshman year public speaking class. My version of this is Do More of What Works.

It's true that social media can take a lot of time and I'm equipping you with the most successful strategies to save you time!

Because Pinterest is beautiful I've accidentally spent way too many hours pinning non- relevant content that didn't deliver leads but I do have a way to know exactly what is working.

My favorite tool for this is Tailwind App. When you create an account, Tailwind will pull your Pinterest analytics into the dashboard. From the dashboard you can see basic information like the number of repins, likes, and new followers within the past week but they have two other tools I can't resist.

The first is Trending Pins. This shows what people

are pinning from your website, who is pinning it and how many people pinned it. Pretty fascinating!

The second must use tool is Pin Inspector. The inspectors pulls a list of pins images you've pinned in the last week and tells you how many times it has been repinned.

Let's just say this is outstanding information to guide you to do more of what is working.

The Art of the Instagram & Iconosquare

Instagram is gorgeous and I love it for so many reasons, but I do something different than you might think.

There's no better way to promote your small business than showing happy customers your product. Instagram is so loved that your customers are freely and willingly posting photos of themselves or their friends using your product.

I love to pull these images into the rest of the social strategy so that people on your blog, your Facebook page and Pinterest page can see this.

For this, I use a simple tool called Iconosquare.

Once your account is created, use the search bar to search for your hashtag or handle. You might be surprised with how many photos there already are!

Next, pull those to your desktop and then post to your other sites. Be sure to tag the person who took the photo for credit and extra exposure!

Engagement:

Strengthen the core of your social success by using best practices that get customers involved.

Right before the ball dropped this year, I noticed all of my friends were declaring their theme for the year on Facebook. The theme is supposed to frame everything you do to help you live more closely attached to that theme. Of course I did this for myself, but I couldn't help but think in terms of social media. This year's social media theme is Engagement. In everything you do on social media for your business work to get more people talking and interacting.

Endless Ways to Create Content on the Fly

Shark Tank broke prime time records with 3.5 million unique viewers on a night in January!

We may not have ever expected people to be so "in" to small businesses pitching their brand as the mass public is, but the truth is that these stories engage audiences, they inspire us to go for our dreams, and they make us believe that the American Dream is a possibility. We love to take a peek behind the curtain. We love to get a few insider tips from experts but there's no doubt that running a your business makes for a busy day and the last thing you want to focus on is "What should I post on Facebook today?"

I'll make this easy for you. Small businesses are one of the best places to find original engaging content and where content can be created on the fly, truly in a few minutes a day.

Start by doing just one or two of these things a day. Be sure you snap a photo with Instagram and have the photo feed directly to your brand's social sites. (These examples are geared toward restaurants and will get you thinking if you're in another industry).

We Eat with Our Eyes

- Menu items

- Daily/Weekly features
- Pastry case
- Sample plate
- Amuse bousche
- Wine flights
- Coffee brewing
- Drinks being poured
- Martinis shaken
- Happy Hour item
- Espresso brewing
- Muddling
- Bread on a sheet rack
- Drinks on a tray
- Your specialty
- Hot plates coming out

Secrets of a Chef

- Chef taste testing
- Sauce simmering
- Ingredients boiling
- Hot food coming out of the oven
- Ingredients going in a bowl
- Chopping
- Flambe
- Blanch
- Bake
- Roast
- Saute
- Steam
- Poach
- Favorite cookbooks
- Chef inspiration

Behind the Scenes

- Staff wine tastings
- New hire training
- New server on the floor
- Opening bottles
- Staff ready for shift
- Corks from the night
- Patio seating
- Music being played
- Decor elements
- Happy guests
- Recipe card
- Liquor room
- Wine cellar
- Team birthdays
- Staff in action
- Host answering phone

- Ringing in gift cards

Around Town

- Charity events
- Galas
- Bridal fairs
- Local "Best Of" lists
- Restaurant shows
- Food and wine expos
- Local press

Love Your Neighbors

- Happy babies
- Kids being cute
- Thank you cards that are sent to you
- Kid's artwork
- Sunrise
- Sunset

- Local landmarks
- Neighborhood festivals

The Happening Spot

- Wine dinners
- Cooking classes
- Happy hour
- Lunch meetings
- A cheers
- A proposal
- Catering leaving
- Birthday celebrations

Emotions not Promotions

- Gift card
- New menu cards
- Wine list
- Drink menu

- Chalkboard features

- Call to action

- Packaging food to go

- The front door

- Online reservation form

- Online private party form

Get Instagram Now

100 million monthly active users. 40 million photos per day. 8,500 likes per second. 1,000 comments per second. Instragram is more than a cool way to take a pictures. It's a way to brand your small business. It's a way to engage with your customers and potential customers. It's a way to stay top of mind.

By now, you're probably well aware of Instagram even if you haven't used it yourself, you've probably seen your customers pulling out their phones and snapping up gorgeous photos of your creations to share on the social network.

It comes as no surprise that this is a platform that you should be paying attention to.

Getting Started

- Create an Instagram account. Make sure to create your Instagram account sooner rather than later to ensure you'll have the best chances of grabbing the account name that best represents your brand.
- Pick your Hashtags. Hashtags are used to group photos and make them easily searchable on Instagram. For example, a customer can click on a hashtag that is associated with a photo of your brand and see other photos of it that have been tagged.
- Establish a clear set of hashtags that you'd like to associate with your brand. These can be anything from your most well-known product or service to your small business' "why." Make your brand irresistible and snap away!

Photo Ideas

- Help customers remember great products, tips and upcoming events by providing them with unique hashtags that they can use to identify them and share with friends.
- Encourage users to share their Instagram photos and your brand's hashtags across their Facebook and Twitter profiles to maximize exposure to potential customers.
- Ask staff to take photos of their preparation

process or product sourcing adventures.

- Giving customers an inside view of your small business, beyond your Shop page, helps to build your brand and get them excited about their next buy!

Customer Insights

- Instagram allows you to track the number of likes, comments, and shares that your photos are receiving, and how often your hashtags are being used but if you want to dig deeper use Iconosquare. Iconosquare will tell you which filter performs best, which dayparts are strongest and your most popular content.

Remember that the goal is to communicate to your customers through images, not just to create unnecessary posts.

30 Ways to Create Fans from Scratch

You know your business should leverage social networks, but its daunting when you have zero followers, zero fans, zero members, zero connections. The good news about social networks is we all start at zero, so even those businesses with thousands of followers now, sat and stared at those big zeros too. The key to getting fans is to get your business "out there." Where ever you are, you just have to start and here is a list of 30 strategies that get impressive results when you need to create fans from scratch.

Attract

- Craft a contagious profile. In 160 characters, people decide if they want to follow you or not. Make it wow!
- Post pictures, tag them and ask for comments or captions. Pictures highly like-able and share-able.
- Post videos and ask for comments and shares. Videos are compelling!

Integrate

- Create a twitter background that gets opt ins. Add your web address and blog url in the left panel so people know other places to find you.
- Include a link to your website in you Facebook About box.
- Add hot links to your website and blog in your Twitter profile.
- Use links on email blasts that take readers to your social networks.
- Incorporate your Twitter handle and Facebook page in your email signature

Give

- Guest post on bigger blogs. Use twitter to help build buzz. Tag the blog in your original post so their followers see it. The day that it goes live, be sure to search it on twitter and respond to every person who replied or retweeted it.
- Guest post on teleseminars and webinars.
- Comment on blogs where your customers are spending their time.
- Reply to every comment you receive.
- Reply to @mentions.
- Write a testimonial for someone else.
- Do a vendor case study.
- Say yes to every interview or writing request.
- Profile other people on your site and make them look fab. They'll be sharing that link for sure!

Partner/Collaborate
- Look for ways to partner with competitors and pitch it. What else does your target customer want? What do you offer that your competitor doesn't?
- Look for ways to partner with big shots and pitch it. What can you add to their offerings?

Promote

- Have a pay-what-you-can-day. Post it everywhere and ask that people share your link.
- Hold a contest. Offer your product or service in exchange for testimonials. Tell people they get bonus points for sharing your contest on their social networks.

Engage
- Start commenting on other blogs.
- Build relationships instead of self promoting.
- Ask questions with simple answers. What's one word to describe (your industry)?

Encourage
- Tell people you're up to something new and encourage them to tell others. Give links and make it easy.
- Call in favors. Ask your friends to share what you are working on. Again, give links and make it easy.
- Do live speaking engagements. Ask people to tweet and post in real time about the event and include your twitter handle or tag your business.
- Put calls to action on everything.
- Ask for testimonials.

- Keep posting. You'll simply remind people you are there.

Facebook and Twitter give incredible opportunity to get your business "out-there." Incorporate a few of these strategies when and where you can.

The Keep in Touch Formula

Keeping in touch with clients and prospects is crucial. Twenty years ago, sales people would make notes about people's hobbies and family on the back of business cards. Now, with social media it's so easy to keep in touch and stay top of mind. I use Facebook and Twitter Lists to keep up on client's and prospect's personal life and interest.

Here's my little Keep-in-Touch formula.

Before reaching out to a prospect, I look at their Facebook profile put them on a Twitter List.

I look at their Facebook profile to see what commonalities we have personally. Do they have kids? Did we go to the same school? Did we live in the same city? Do we like similar music? Do we have similar hobbies? When I send an initial email, I make sure that I open with the sentence about our commonality to warm it up and start building an authentic connection with them.

Twitter Lists have been so amazing for opening doors to people I wouldn't otherwise be able to have direct conversation with. Once the prospect or client is on my Twitter List, I look for was to jump into their conversation. It might be professional or personal but the goal is to get my name in front of them and to start a relationship. After we've had a few conversations on Twitter and I think that this person would recognize my name in an email, I send that email. In the first sentence I always reference our conversation on Twitter to remind them just in case. This is the exact formula I used to connect with an editor for HGTV and how I landed a spot on HGTV.com!

As a keep in touch (and stay top of mind) technique, I friend them on Facebook and look for ways to have authentic conversations. I look for things I can give them. Do they have a question that I can answer? Are they looking for an introduction to someone I know?

Then, I look for ways to celebrate their life and successes, by congratulating them on product launches, big sales boosts, speaking engagements and even personal things like kid's birthdays, their birthday and anniversary, family vacations and even the little things like making Christmas cookies.

Get More Facebook Engagement

Did you know that a green light once meant STOP? Did you also know that pink was the color for baby boys? That's a little confusing.

Social media best practices are constantly changing and can be confusing too, but here is a list of 5 tested social media tactics for getting more likes, comments and shares on Facebook!

5 Proven Secrets for More Engagement

- Fill in the blank. They are simple and guests are compelled to give their own word input.
- Call to Action. It's marketing 101, but consumers need to be told what to do. Click like. Share this. Comment below.
- Ask What and When, not Why and How. Research shows that when your fans can respond with simple easy to come up with answers engagement will be higher than when they need to give significant thought to a response.
- Great Photos. The amount of social media real estate that a post with an image is given compared to the amount of real estate a post without an image makes it obvious why image posts

perform 53% better than non-image posts.
- Double Whammy Post. Use an image and a link to your website where they can make an online reservation or reserve their seat for an upcoming event. Lead people through your process like restaurants lead guests through each course.

Pinterest Boards for So-Called Non-Visual Brands

Product brands are certainly easy to promote on Pinterest but I hear grumbling when I recommend that a service based business leverage Pinterest. The common thread behind the grumbling is: what will I pin?

No sweat, I have a big list to get you started!

• Trendspotting

• First timer tools and resources

• Feature your clients and what they do

• People your service could benefit

• Your services, sessions & conferences

- Press, interviews & places you've been featured
- Inspiration behind what you do
- Your portfolio, blogs, podcasts & videos
- Your clients' lifestyle interests
- Speaking engagements
- Quotes
- Events to attend
- Other service providers you recommend
- Your team
- Your team's interests
- Great articles for your audience
- Your affiliates
- Helpful how to's
- Blogs worth following
- Books that make an impact
- Events to attend

- Things relevant to what you do

- Great ebooks

- Outstanding webinars & online trainings

Pinterest Boards to Create

Just like learning to ride a bike, sometimes you need a little push to get started. If you have a product based business, start with these types of boards!

Baby/Kids

- Fashion trends

- Delicious kid friendly recipes

- Learning activities

- New statistics parents need to know

- Celebrity style

- Tips for parents

- Kid friendly apps and websites

- Crafts & projects for your little ones

- Cute & clever kids room ideas

Fashion

- Color trends & inspiration
- Style boards
- Fashion bloggers worth following
- Spot on stylists
- Perfect accessories
- Hair how to's
- Your product line
- Best retailers with your line
- Celebrity inspiration
- Make up trick and tips
- Outstanding shopping destinations
- Your process & behind the scenes

Food

- Favorite recipes using your product
- Top restaurants

- Outstanding grocery and boutique health stores

- Kitchen gadgets

- Helpful how to's

- Spotlight chefs

- Behind the scenes

- Taste testing

- Gorgeous food shots

- Favorite local destination for foodies

- Magazines and blogs worth reading

- Table set ups

Training:

Educate and encourage your team to be actively involved in your online marketing and sales initiative.

One of the biggest steps in my business was to trust my baby business in the hands of others. I put off hiring for many reasons: not enough revenue coming in, trust, too much time to train and more. When I finally got past my fear that the company would fail if I asked for help, I soared. This team is incredible, whip smart and on it!

Suddenly, I'm able to do so much more and make a bigger impact.

My advice to you is to ask your team for help with your online and social media marketing efforts (or outsource it to a partner).

Social Media Team Guidelines

You probably really trust your team, but just like having contracts in place, it's important to have social media guidelines in place. Afterall, what is being posted via social networks is out there, visible and frames your brand!

Here's a template to help you set up your guidelines.

The following guidelines have been established to ensure understanding and adherence to Padron Social Marketings' social media usage policy. Social media projects are owned by Padron Social Marketings' including: content, artwork, photography, interviews, and future usage. Social media champions agree to uphold the company/brand standards, represent Padron Social Marketings' in a favorable light and maintain ongoing contact with Padron Social Marketings' social media staff. In the event of separation of employment from Padron Social Marketings', administrative access will be revoked.

Employees may not send or receive messages in violation of federal and state law, in violation of Company policy, in violation of the property or copyright interest of another, or in any inappropriate discriminatory or unauthorized manner. Use of Company-provided resources in violation of this policy may result in disciplinary action, up to and including termination.

- *Use good judgment. Refrain from comments that can be interpreted as discriminatory, harassing, slurs, demeaning or inflammatory. If you are in a situation that you are unsure how to handle, stop and contact Katrina Padron for help.*

- *Consider your audience. When you are on Padron Social Marketings' social media networks, remember that your readers include current clients and potential clients.*

- *Protect confidential and proprietary information. Be transparent without giving away confidential information such as sales information and new products being developed.*

- *Use admin log-in. Each time you are posting Padron Social Marketings' page log in as yourself, then select "Use Facebook as Page."*

- *Be responsible for what you write and do. Use good judgment and common sense.*

- *Be authentic. Include your name and your title when appropriate. Guests want to know and trust you.*

- *Share your ideas for campaigns, deals, coupons or special promotions by emailing katrina@padronsocialmarketing.com. ALL posts that have an associated cost attached must be approved by Katrina prior to posting. We will try to work your ideas into future plans.*

- *Bring value. Make recommendations. Forward complaints and concerns to katrina@padronsocialmarketing.com to address.*

- *Be productive. Stay focused on your main job functions. Try to work in just 5 minutes a day for Facebook; it is not meant to replace your current responsibilities.*

I have read and understand the guidelines.

Name: _____

Date: _____

7 Steps to Create a Powerhouse Social Media Team

Social media can seem overwhelming. Let's face it, if you are running a business, you are really busy running the business, right? Have you ever thought, "I just want someone else to do it for me!" You're in luck. Just like other projects in your business you can train your staff to use social media to create relationships with your customers and get your business out there.

Here's everything you need to know about getting your team ready for the social media front lines.

Start with a recruiting session. Depending on the

size of your team, you might be able to hand select this team or you could ask for input from your managers. Be strategic. Look for passionate, tech savvy people who are skilled communicators.

Tell people what you are doing and why. Try a script like this.

Our vision for 2014 is to reach out to more fans, build partnerships and attract more people to our brand. We are getting on Facebook and are looking for passionate, tech savvy team members who want to join us.

Plan a training session. When you have a handful of people committed to your social media team, schedule a training session. These meetings are most effective when everyone can see the same screen. If your team is local, your training session could be done in training room with your computer screen projected. If that is not an option, use an online webinar service provider with screen sharing options. The best free resource for screen sharing is Skype or anymeeting.com.

Create your presentation. Cover each of these topics.

- Your purpose. The most effective way to use social media is to build relationships with your customers. Your purpose might be to create a community of fans who love what you do and happily spread the good word.

- Set frequency expectations. Plan to have a few posts each day. Depending on the size of your team that might mean that one person posts one time per day or maybe just a couple times a week.
- Set content expectations. The biggest social media question is "I'm on Facebook and Twitter, what do I say?" You really have to know your target customer but use "e-cubed." E-cubed is educate, empower and entertain. Consider your ideal target fan and brainstorm posts that they would find educational, empowering and entertaining.
  - You are a commercial interior designer. Your target is decision maker at a development company. They might find "how 'green' design innovations are impacting the bottom line" educational and empowering. Post that.
  - You have an antique furniture shop. Your target is an interior designer. It might be entertaining and educational to know the history of the piece or it

might be empowering to know how to restore the piece. Post that.

- Determine your ratio between relationship building and self promotion. A common issue to address beforehand is how much relationship building posts you want in comparison to how much self promotion would you like to see. I recommend the 80/20 rule – 80% relationship building and 20% self promotion. That ratio will help you achieve your goal of creating communities of fans who love what you do and happily spread the good word.

- Give admin access. Giving your team members admin access will allow your team to create posts as your business rather than their personal profile. Your fans will only see your business profile picture instead of the individual person's picture. If you would like to know who the post came from and to encourage ownership, ask your team to type "- their name" after each post. To set up admin access you will need their personal email address that they use to login to Facebook and they will need to "Like" your business' Facebook page.

- Develop your Social Media Guidelines.

Require that every team member read, sign and adhere to your established social media guidelines. You are allowing your team members to communicate with fans on your behalf and want to make sure they uphold the brand standards, represent your business in a favorable light and maintain ongoing contact with you regarding concerns or progress.

- You are busy running your business. Put these steps in action to lead your team to your social media goals: reach out to more fans, build partnerships and attract more people to our brand.

www.ingramcontent.com/pod-product-compliance
Lightning Source LLC
Chambersburg PA
CBHW071721170526
45165CB00005B/2103